THE
RIGHTS
AND
WRONGS
OF

anger

H. NORMAN
WRIGHT

HARVEST HOUSE PUBLISHERS
Eugene, Oregon 97402

THE RIGHTS AND WRONGS OF ANGER

Copyright © 1985 by Harvest House Publishers
Eugene, Oregon 97402

Library of Congress Catalog Card Number 85-60129
ISBN 0-89081-457-0

Printed in the United States of America.

CONTENTS

THE
RIGHTS
AND
WRONGS
OF

anger

1

THE FRUSTRATION FEELING

Frustrated! No matter what you want to do, no matter what you try, nothing seems to work.

Frustration is an inevitable human feeling. It is a condition of wanting something and not getting it. Frustration can occur when our goals or desires are blocked. It can also be just the opposite—when we don't want something but have it forced upon us.

Frustration can also be related to expectations. When we do a kind act for someone, we expect it to be recognized and even reciprocated. When this expectation is not fulfilled, frustration and then anger can occur. In fact, frustration and anger are closely related much of the time.

Have you ever—
  • worn yourself out cleaning the house

all day, but no one noticed your efforts?

- spent two hours fixing yourself up, hoping he would notice and perhaps suggest going out to dinner, but nothing happened?

- brought your wife a surprise gift (an expensive one, at that) and then saw no excitement on her face?

- worked for days on a project, but the boss took it for granted and never even thanked you?

- taken the kids on a special outing, but all they did was bicker and fight?

- left an hour early to avoid the rush-hour traffic just to discover that thousands of other motorists did the same thing?

- wanted to share your excitement over a new experience you had that day, but your spouse and children weren't interested?

- had a day off and wanted to sleep in, but you woke up bright and early and couldn't get back to sleep?

You probably have your own list of frustrations. Take a few minutes right now and write down 12 situations which frustrate you the most. After you have done that, write down how you usually respond to those frustrations.

_____

_____

_____

_____

_____

_____

_____

_____

_____

_____

_____

_____

_____

2

HANDLING
FRUSTRATION

Now that you have considered your own frustrations, let's consider a popular myth about frustration: *Frustration always upsets a person!* That is not true. Frustration does not always make a person upset, disturbed, or angry! It depends upon the individual. If we think and plan carefully before a frustrating situation occurs, our predetermined course of action can help us avoid an anger reaction. So much of our disturbance and anger can be attributed to our thought life and our expectations. *It is possible to accept frustrations without becoming upset.*

Dr. Paul Hauck, a psychotherapist, put it this way:

> Millions of frustrations are far more easily tolerated than we usually think. Children not finishing their dinner is not an awful

10

frustration, just the waste of a few cents. And if a few cents bothers you, put the plate in the refrigerator until later. A person swerving in front of you in traffic is not doing something that calls for a nuclear explosion. It isn't awful to have someone honking his horn impolitely behind you—it's only slightly annoying. Not getting your raise can hurt your pocketbook but not you, unless you let it. . . . Frustrations are not usually earth-shaking to begin with—they can be tolerated quite nicely if we make the effort. Secondly, frustrations, even if they *are* severe, don't have to lead to disturbances unless we allow them to.[1]

One way to handle frustration is to accept it as being as inevitable as death. Frustrations are a part of life. Why be so surprised when they occur? You can choose to look at a frustration as a catastrophe or as an opportunity for growth. It is your own choice.

The word "frustration" is derived from the Latin word *frustra*, which means "in vain." A dictionary definition of frustration is "a sense of insecurity or dissatisfaction arising from unresolved problems or unfulfilled needs." We are frustrated when we face a problem but can find no solution to it.

Harold Walker describes frustration as "the experience of blundering into dead-end streets and blind alleys and getting nowhere for all our trying. You and I may as well face the blunt fact of frustration as one of life's inevitables. There is no escape from it, and sooner or later we are caught in its grip.[2]

Sometimes when we become frustrated we are really saying to ourselves, "I've failed." We interpret not getting what we want as failure. During the 1976 Olympic Games in Montreal there were two examples of response to failure. Two young British sailors actually set fire to their yacht when they came in fourteenth in a field of sixteen! They left it burning and then waded ashore. Their attitudes reflected something more than just defeat. Yet Olneus Charles of Haiti, who ran in the 10,000-meter race, didn't come close to winning. He was lapped nine times in the race and finished five minutes behind everyone else, but he didn't quit or become frustrated. He failed in the race but not in his attitude.

Too often when we let failure bring on frustration we look for a culprit—someone to blame and at whom we can vent our feelings.

Many of the events which frustrate us have been blown out of proportion. We magnify what has occurred and literally create mountains out of molehills. Little annoyances sometimes activate our frustration button. But annoyances are a part of life. Accepting them and giving them permission to be there can relieve some of the pressure. Even looking for the humor of a situation can ease pressure.

Part of the problem of frustration is that it is a form of stress which can have a detrimental effect upon the body. An organism that has a continual level of stress wears down faster. It becomes an easy target of medical problems which are related to stress. And frustration leads to anger and hostility. Gary Collins says that—

> Whenever people get frustrated, they have a tendency to respond with aggression. This aggression can be of two types. Sometimes we react overtly, lashing out with our tongues or with our fists. This is like blowing our horn at the train. Such behavior isn't usually acceptable in polite society, so it is more common for us to react passively. Here we may smile and be charming on the outside while we seethe with anger inside and look for more subtle ways to express ourselves.[3]

3

THE BIBLE AND FRUSTRATION

An example of frustration in Scripture is found in 1 Samuel. Achish, King of Gath, gave David the ancient city of Ziklag. But while David and his men were away, the city was invaded and destroyed by the Amalekites and the people taken captive. Because they were so frustrated by their losses, David's men spoke of stoning him. The Bible says, "David was greatly distressed...but David encouraged himself in the Lord his God" (1 Samuel 30:6 KJV). David could have given up in despair, but he made another choice: He found a solution.

The Scripture provides some insight into the problem of frustration. Several passages indicate the proper response that we should have to frustration.

"Consider it wholly joyful, my brethren, whenever you are enveloped in or encounter trials of any sort, or fall into various temptations. Be assured and understand that the trial and proving of your faith bring out endurance and steadfastness and patience" (James 1:2,3 AMP).

"[You should] be exceedingly glad on this account, though now for a little while you may be distressed by trials and suffer temptations, so that [the genuineness] of your faith may be tested" (1 Peter 1:6,7 AMP).

"Blessed, happy, to be envied is the man who is patient under trial and stands up under temptation, for when he has stood the test and been approved he will receive [the victor's] crown of life which God has promised to those who love Him" (James 1:12 AMP).

Many temptations are frustrations, and some frustrations can become temptation to sin. But the Word of God indicates the attitude we should have in these situations.

4

THE SOURCE OF FRUSTRATION

Frustration occurs in many forms. You may experience frustration in the area of your wishes, desires, ambitions, hopes, hungers, instincts, or even your will. You may often respond with anger. If you are hungry and cannot eat, you may become angry. If you are frightened by something and cannot run away, you may become angry. If you want to join a certain club and cannot, you may become angry.

When you are frustrated, you must consider the source of your frustration. Objects, situations, or other people may be the cause. Your friends, father, mother, wife, husband, children, or employer could be the source of frustration. You can be frustrated just as easily by someone you dislike as by the one you love the most.

You could also be frustrated by what some

16

people call the laws of nature. If you are hungry, you could be frustrated by an empty refrigerator. If you have looked forward to playing tennis on your first day off in three weeks and it rains on that day, you could be disappointed and frustrated.

Even your values or moral system can frustrate you and deter you from fulfilling certain desires. Some Christians have been heard to say, "If only I weren't a Christian I could do that and really enjoy it!" Even though this person wants to retain his value system, it can be very frustrating. Sometimes we tend to blame God for our frustration because we feel that He places too many limitations upon us or does not give us what we think we deserve.

5

FRUSTRATION AND ANGER

Why does frustration lead to anger? The basic assumptions that we have about life can cause anger to arise out of frustration. Frustration may begin with the desire for something: "I want something." Desires are natural; we all have wants and desires. We set goals and we want them to come true. But we must distinguish between "I want something" and *"I must have it."* If we can distinguish between the two, we may not become so upset.

When we say "I want something" we are sometimes saying, "I must have it. I've got to have it or else. If I don't get it, the result is going to be awful. I've got to have my way, and if anyone blocks me he is terrible. In fact, if he doesn't let me get my way, then that's just a sign that he doesn't love me." These statements only help create anger within us.

18

We assume that we *must* have our way, and we are frustrated because this should not happen to us.

Perhaps we should ask the question, "Why not?" Why shouldn't we experience frustration just like everyone else? We are not immune from it, and it can become a growth experience for us if we lengthen the initial statement: "I want something, *but it is all right if I don't get it*. It is not the end of the world. I can live without it and can adjust and find an alternative."

Learning to live without something can often bring a greater level of satisfaction to our lives. This is not to say that we should totally give up and never forge ahead. It is just that we should not allow ourselves to become upset by the various frustrations of life. If we do, the result is an emotional response which most people call anger.

Many of our frustrations can be linked to our self-talk. You and I carry on conversations with ourselves, and this is very normal. Self-talk is a message that you tell yourself. It is a set of evaluating thoughts about facts and events which happen to you. By your self-talk you can create a state of anger and depression or else peace and joy.

Let's consider two potentially frustrating situations and the self-talk which occurs from them.

Situation 1: The house is a mess, especially the kitchen. Jim's wife is gone, and he decides he is going to treat his wife by cleaning the living room, family room, and kitchen. He vacuums, sweeps, dusts, and washes dishes for two hours. "Wait until she sees this. Will she be surprised! She'll go wild with appreciation." So he hopes.

Sometime later his wife, Mary, arrives home with bags of groceries and clothes. She staggers into the house and drops the bags in the living room.

"Jim, would you bring in some of the groceries for me, please? There are so many and I'm beat. Wait until you see the great prices I found on clothes at May Company. And guess who I saw..."

And so it goes for the next hour. Mary never mentions one word about the clean rooms. And after her whirlwind entrance, the house soon looks like a hurricane had swept through. By now Jim is doing a slow burn. His anger has reached the boiling point. Is it her behavior that creates Jim's anger? Or is it his own thoughts? Let's enter his mind to see what he is thinking.

"She should have noticed all this work I did for her."

"She should have thanked me."

"She shouldn't have been so insensitive and inconsiderate."

"What a lousy way to treat me."

"She shouldn't have messed up these rooms."

"Just wait until she wants me to help her! Fat chance."

Jim's thoughts are making him feel hurt and angry. He could have thought:

"I wish she would notice the work I've done."

"Perhaps I did all this for what I would get out of it instead of just helping her."

"I can get along without her noticing. If not, I'll just ask if she noticed anything. I could let her know I have a better understanding of what housework is like."

"Next time I'll find a creative way to let her know her work has been done for her."

This series of thoughts is more realistic and less emotionally charged. Changing "should" statements to "I wish..." or "It would be nice if..." will help us to use our minds to control our emotions so we can maintain the ability to reason.

Situation 2: Jack was frustrated when he

came in for counseling. He was livid with anger at his wife. "You bet I'm angry!" he said. "I've got a right to be. If you had to live with a hypocritical woman you'd be angry too. Of course, she puts on a great performance. She responds with love, kindness, patience, and fairness with everyone else. But at home it's just the opposite! Everyone at church sees her as a saint. Ha! At home she's constantly griping, complaining, running me down, and comparing me to others. If there's a fault to be found with me, she'll find it. She makes life miserable for me, and I'm burned up. And don't tell me I don't have a right to be angry. I'm ready to take a walk on her!"

Jack had many expectations for Celeste which (from his point of view) were not being fulfilled.

As we talked we discovered that Jack not only had expectations but felt he had a right to demand that she fulfill those expectations. Jack was telling himself that:

1. It is wrong and terrible to be treated by my wife in this way, especially when she demonstrates Christian love to others.

2. I am correct in demanding that she treats me differently than she does.

3. She owes me love and a submissive attitude, since she is my wife.

4. She is terrible to treat me this way.

5. She should change her response to me.

Jack's self-talk and expectations were creating his anger. As we continued to explore his feelings we discovered that he felt like he was wasting his life with Celeste and that he wasn't sure she could change. He believed that (most of the time) he was loving, kind, and considerate with Celeste and that she should respond in like manner.

Jack had three causes for his anger: 1) expectations; 2) a list of shoulds and oughts for Celeste; 3) a pattern of self-talk which fed his anger.

Listed below are five statements that people have made indicating their wants or desires. Space is provided for you to write a response to each statement. Your response should help you accept the possibility of the particular desire not being fulfilled.

For example, "I want my husband to notice the clean house that I've spent seven hours slaving over today." If the husband doesn't notice the clean house, the wife may either give him the cold shoulder or a Vesuvian eruption over his lack of sensitivity, consideration, and appreciation.

The following statement might help the wife to accept her husband's lack of appreciation:

"I want my husband to notice the clean house that I've spent seven hours slaving over today. But if he doesn't, that's all right too. My happiness and sense of satisfaction do not depend on his response. I didn't clean it up solely for his response but because it needed to be cleaned. I feel better about the house and my effort. His appreciation would just be an added benefit."

Under each statement below, write a response that you could make to yourself in your own mind that would help you accept the frustration.

1. "I need to get to the sale at the store before everything is picked over. It's my only opportunity to save that much money."

_____

_____

_____

_____

_____

_____

_____

2. "I sure hope dinner is ready when I get home tonight and the kids keep quiet for a

change. I don't need any hassle today."

_____

_____

_____

_____

_____

_____

3. "After all the work I've put in on that committee, I hope I'm considered for the chairmanship this year. It means a lot to me to be able to lead that group."

_____

_____

_____

_____

_____

_____

4. "I've just got to get this work done today before our guests arrive. I don't know what I'll do if they arrive before I finish."

_____

_____

_____

_____

_____

_____

_____

5. "After giving my son piano lessons for seven years and paying all that money, I certainly hope he doesn't ask to quit. Last year at this time he really hassled me about it. I just don't need that."

_____

_____

_____

_____

_____

_____

_____

Now consider another step that can lessen the amount of frustration you experience. When you want something, do you let other people know about it or is it an unspoken expectation? Other people are not mind-readers and will not know what you want unless you share it with them. Telling the children or your spouse what you expect assists them in meeting your needs. Often they are grateful because you brought your desires out into the open. If they don't respond as you expected, you don't have to become angry. You can learn to adjust and adapt. You can also learn to communicate your needs to them in a clearer and more positive manner. This will increase the likelihood of your desires being fulfilled. If one approach doesn't work, try another.

Life is full of frustrations and irritations. One of my favorite writers is Chuck Swindoll. In his excellent book *Growing Strong in the Seasons of Life* he talks about the daily irritations of life. Let's consider some of his thoughts from a chapter titled "The String of Pearls":

> ...make a mental list of some of the things that irritate you. Here are a few suggestions that will get you started:

traffic jams	cold food
talkative people	interruptions
long lines	reminders
crying babies	deadlines
phone calls	nosy neighbors
misplaced keys	being rushed
untrained pets	late planes
stuck zippers	tight clothes
squeaking doors	incompetence
flat tires	balancing checkbooks
doing dishes	mothers-in-law
weeds	high prices
peeling onions	

Any of those make you want to grind your teeth? Some of it sounds like today, doesn't it? It's easy to get the feeling that you can't win—no matter how hard you try. . . .

If it weren't for irritations we'd be very patient, wouldn't we? We could wade calmly through life's placid sea and never encounter a ripple. Unfortunately, irritations comprise the major occupational hazard of the human race. One of these days it should dawn upon our minds that we'll never be completely free from irritations as long as we tread Planet Earth. Never. Upon arriving at such a profound conclusion, it would be wise to consider an alternative to losing our cool. The secret is *adjusting*.

Sure, that sounds simple. But it isn't. Several things tend to keep us on the ulcerated edge of irritability. If we lived in the zoo, the sign outside our cage might read: "Human Being—Creature of Habit." We tend to develop habit reactions, wrong though they may be. We are also usually in a hurry. . . inordinately wedded to the watch on our wrist. Furthermore, many of our expectations for the day are unrealistic. Echoing in our heads are the demanding voices of objectives that belong to a *week*, rather than a single day. All of this makes the needle on our inner pressure gauge whirl like Mario Andretti's tachometer. When you increase the heat to our highly pressurized system by a fiery irritation or two. . . or three. . . BOOM! Off goes the lid and out comes the steam.

It helps me if I remember that God is in charge of my day...not I. While He is pleased with the wise management of time and intelligent planning from day to day, He is mainly concerned with the development of inner character. He charts growth toward maturity, concerning Himself with the cultivation of priceless, attractive qualities that make us Christlike down deep within. One of His preferred methods of training us is through adjustment to irritation.[4]

6

ANGER

Since frustration may cause anger, we ought to consider exactly what we mean by anger. A dictionary definition of anger is "a strong, usually temporary feeling of displeasure." But this does not specify the manner of anger's expressions. You can be just as angry while keeping silent as you can while yelling at someone.

The words *rage* and *fury* are used to describe intense, uncontained, explosive emotion. Fury is thought of as being destructive, but rage can be considered justified by certain circumstances.

Another word for anger is *wrath*—fervid anger that seeks vengeance or punishment. *Resentment* is usually used to signify suppressed anger brought about by a sense of grievance. *Indignation* is a feeling which results when you see the mistreatment of someone or something that is very important to you.

Rage interferes with our growth and our relationships. It produces attacks (verbal or physical), tantrums, and revenge; it can destroy other people first and then ourselves.

Resentment is another loser. It breeds bitterness and creates passive-aggressive responses. Resentment can actually destroy us and, in time, other people as well.

Resentment is a cancerous growth produced by unresolved anger. It is a feeling of indignant displeasure or persistent ill will of something regarded as a wrong, insult, or injury.

Resentment creates a filter through which you view the person whom you resent. You develop a flair for finding flaws in whatever the other person says or does. Any difficulties which occur in your relationship are attributed to the other person. Your energy is now diverted into blame. You may also continue to save and store your irritations, thereby creating even more resentment.

Since we are rational creatures we can choose how we will respond to external events. In fact we have more control than we give ourselves credit for. Often our past experiences, memories, and patterns of response tend to hinder us from exercising this control, but we can overcome these influences.

. In his book on anger, Richard Walters compares the effects of all three: rage, resentment, and indignation.

> Rage seeks to do wrong, resentment seeks to hide wrong, indignation seeks to correct wrong.
>
> Rage and resentment seek to destroy people, indignation seeks to destroy evil.
>
> Rage and resentment seek vengeance, indignation seeks justice.
>
> Rage is guided by selfishness, resentment is guided by cowardice, indignation is guided by mercy.
>
> Rage uses open warfare, resentment is a guerrilla fighter, indignation is an honest and fearless and forceful defender of truth.
>
> Rage defends itself, resentment defends the status quo, indignation defends the other person.
>
> Rage and resentment are forbidden by the Bible, indignation is required.[5]
>
> Rage blows up the bridges people need to reach each other, and resentment sends people scurrying behind barriers to hide from each other and to hurt each other indirectly. Indignation is constructive: it seeks to heal hurts and to bring people together. Its purpose is to rebuild the bridges and pull down the barriers, yet it is like rage and resentment in that the feeling of anger remains.[6]

Neil Warren has suggested that anger is a dangerous emotion.

> It is common knowledge that:
> – If you pretend you have no anger and try to bury it, it can bury you—literally—by triggering a heart attack or a stroke.
>
> – If you let it out in the wrong way, it can ruin your marriage, alienate your children, or get you fired.
>
> – If you somehow get it turned around on yourself, it can tear your self-image apart, destroy your self-esteem, and set you up for all kinds of psychic pain.
>
> – If you fail to process it when you experience it, it may turn to resentment; and if it does, you can become hostile, negative, and impossible to be around.[7]

7

THE BIBLE AND ANGER

The Word of God has much to say about anger, and uses a number of words to describe the various types of anger. In the Old Testament the word for anger actually meant "nostril" or "nose." In ancient Hebrew symbolism the nose was pictured as the seat of anger. The phrase "slow to anger" literally means "long of nose." Synonyms used in the Old Testament for anger include ill-humor and rage (Esther 1:12), overflowing rage and fury (Amos 1:11), and indignation (Jeremiah 15:17). The emotion of anger can be the subject of the Scripture even though the exact word is not present. Anger can be implied through such words as revenge, cursing, jealousy, snorting, trembling, shouting, raving, and grinding the teeth.

Several words are used for anger in the New Testament. It is important to note the distinction between these words. Many people have concluded that Scripture contradicts itself because in one verse we are taught not to be angry and in another we are admonished to "be angry and sin not." Which is correct and which should we follow?

One of the words used most often for anger in the New Testament is *thumas*. It describes anger as a turbulent commotion or a boiling agitation of feelings. This type of anger blazes up into a sudden explosion. It is an outburst from inner indignation and is similar to a match which ignites quickly into a blaze but then burns out rapidly. This type of anger is mentioned 20 times in such passages as Ephesians 4:31 and Galatians 5:20. We are to control this type of anger.

Another type of anger, mentioned only three times in the New Testament, and never in a positive sense, is *parorgismos*. This is anger that has been provoked. It is characterized by irritation, exasperation, or embitterment.

> . . .do not ever let your wrath—your exasperation, your fury or indignation—last until the sun goes down (Ephesians 4:26 AMP).

> Again I ask, Did Israel not understand? Did the Jews have no warning that the Gospel was to go forth to the Gentiles, to all the earth? First, there is Moses who says, I will make you jealous of those who are not a

nation; with a foolish nation I will make you angry (Romans 10:19 AMP).

The most common New Testament word for anger is *orge*. It is used 45 times and means a more settled and long-lasting attitude which is slower in its onset but more enduring. It often includes revenge. This kind of anger is similar to coals on a barbeque slowly warming up to red-hot and then white-hot and holding this temperature until the cooking is done.

The overall theme of Scripture concerning anger is that it will be a part of life. It is not to be denied, but it is to be controlled. Certain types of anger are not healthy and should be put away. Anger should be aroused against definite injustices and then used properly.

What about the type of anger that you experience? What is it like? How would you classify it as you read over these definitions again? Take a few moments right now to think of some examples of each of these types of anger in your own life. Write down the situation and circumstances, and describe the results of this anger.

Describe how you felt at the time, and the reaction of other people to you.

_____

_____

_____

8

CAUSES OF
ANGER

What are the causes of anger? Unfortunately, the vast majority of people never realize that anger, like depression, is simply a form of message that we are sending to ourselves. Anger is the result of something else occurring within our life; when we can learn to go beyond anger and discover its root cause, we have started on the process of solving our anger difficulties. Anger has these basic causes: *hurt*, *frustration*, and *fear*. Sometimes *injustice* is given as a cause, but it may actually encompass all three.

When a person experiences *hurt*, such as rejection, criticism, or physical or emotional pain, a very normal reaction is *anger*. We strike back and counterattack that which we feel is causing the pain.

Remember when Jesus looked at the Pharisees with anger? The passage stated that He was "grieved at their hardness of heart" (Mark 3:5 NASB). He was hurt.

Another cause of anger is *frustration*. This we have discussed in a previous section, and we know that expectations and self-talk contribute to the anger.

Fear also causes anger. When we are afraid of something, we often do not act afraid, but instead become angry. For some reason anger is more comfortable than fear. Perhaps it is because we are on the offensive rather than on the defensive. *When you are afraid and act in anger you confuse others around you.* You are not telling them what you are really feeling inside, and all they can do is respond to your anger. Unfortunately, in most cases anger begets anger.

Take the example of the husband who is home every night from work at 6:00. One night he is late. 6:40, 7:00, 7:30 go by and not a word from him. All this time his wife is becoming increasingly more worried, concerned, and fearful. She begins thinking that something awful has happened to him. Finally about 8:00 he comes in and announces that he is home and asks if there is any dinner left. Instead of going to him and sharing her fear and concern she responds with "Well, where have you been? You sure are inconsiderate—not letting me know you were going to be late," etc. You can probably think of other situations similar to this.

When you are angry, ask yourself these questions: Do I feel hurt? Am I experiencing frustration over something? What am I frustrated about? Am I afraid of something? Write these questions on a 3 x 5 card and carry it with you to remind you of the real reasons for your anger.

If you are with another person who is angry, instead of becoming angry at his anger, ask him with sensitivity and compassion, "Are you feeling hurt over something right now? Are you frustrated about a situation? Are you in some way afraid?"

Another cause for anger is *blame*. Blame means that we find fault with another person's behavior and with the person at the same time. I'm sure you've heard the statement "hate the sin, but not the sinner." We need to separate the person from his behavior.

Paul Hauck says concerning blame:

> Suppose you hang a picture on the wall with a small nail and the picture falls to the floor a few hours later. Would you blame the picture because it was too heavy for the nail and insist it was an evil picture? Neither, I hope, or you'd be more neurotic than you already suspect you are. What I hope you would do is forget about blaming the picture or the nail and decide what you have to do about the problem. Either get a lighter picture

or a heavier nail. That's being problem-oriented, not blame-oriented. But notice, it is also being fault-oriented. If you don't know what's at fault, you can't very well change the trouble. So being fault-oriented is good and not at all the same as blame-oriented.[8]

You may say, "Well, hanging a picture is one thing, but if you had to put up with my family's behavior, you'd be angry too." Perhaps not. Do we really need to blame people? Is blame what we really want? No! We want the other person *to change his or her behavior*. And blame doesn't do it! Encouraging the person to engage in more positive behavior is far better. Pointing out and dwelling on another person's mistakes and problems tends to reinforce the possibility of the mistakes recurring. If you expect the other person to respond in a negative way which disturbs you, it can be a self-fulfilling prophecy.

An additional cause for anger which is often overlooked is *the desire for power*. Power is not only having control or influence over other people but is also the freedom from being coerced by others. When we feel that our behavior is our own, we feel powerful. But if we feel that our behavior is determined by other people we feel weak and out of control, and we can become angry. Those who are dependent upon other people and care too much about what others think about them have less power and often more anger. And power comes from how we see ourselves, not how we behave.

If you have a strong need to feel powerful, but are thwarted in this, your anger has some effect on the way you relate to other people. For example, if you become angry you gain a sense of power. By being angry you are not that interested in relating to other people in a warm, friendly fashion. Not only that, but other people don't want to relate to you in a warm, friendly way when you are angry at them. Anger keeps the angry person from feeling weak.

Somewhere we have learned that it is bad to feel weak and out of control. But there are so many situations in life when we are going to be out of control. Why not admit it, accept it, and give ourselves permission to be or feel out of control? That very process gives us back a feeling of control.

The sense of power that we receive from anger is actually a false sense of power: It prevents us from growing and building better relationships. It also helps us deny reality!

In marriage, power struggles are quite common. Many arguments which occur between couples are expressions of a power struggle rather than two different viewpoints clashing.

Have you ever been in a situation where

you are trying to get a baby to stop crying or a dog to stop barking, but nothing works? Do you recall how you felt? Was it pleasure, delight, joy? Of course not. You began to feel angry, but before that, deep down inside you there was a fear of being out of control. You didn't have the power you needed to stop the noise. You talked nicely to the child or dog, then you raised your voice, and then you made threats! In some cases physical violence breaks out. Why? Because you want to regain power, and your anger becomes the motivating factor in this effort.

Are some people more prone to anger than others? Let's look at one type of personality which is gaining more and more prominence in our society.

Perhaps you have heard of the Type A personality. This type of personality—

- may be a man *or* a woman.
- is learned and can be changed.
- is three to five times more prone to a heart attack than the average personality.
- is often angry, hostile, and cynical.

Type A individuals have a perceived enemy: time. They have a chronic struggle with time, and their impatience is easily seen. Hurry, hurry, hurry is their byword.

Let's look at the characteristics of the Type

A personality and note the relationship to anger.

1. There is a tendency to overplan. It's one thing to make plans, but Type A's make plans for their plans! They try to cram too much into the allotted time and are usually behind, which creates two responses: frustration/irritation and the hurry-up syndrome. Part of their reasoning is that "I'm successful because I can accomplish things faster than other people." Deliberation is sacrificed for speed. Any unexpected event is a major disruption and a source for anger. Because of the drive to excel, there is a tendency toward perfectionism. This too is thwarted because of the lack of time, and the Type A person becomes dissatisfied with the work he accomplishes.

2. The Type A person has multiple thoughts and actions. He (or she) seems restless. While he is doing one thing, he may be thinking of several others which need tending to at the same time. You would think he went to juggling school! He also rushes others who want to communicate with him. His impatience may reflect his anger. And he speaks rapidly. He seems in a rush to get all the information out.

3. The Type A person needs to win. His

personal happiness appears to be based upon winning. He becomes upset and agitated when he doesn't win. His motto in all areas of life is "Win at any cost." Watch out if he doesn't!

4. Another characteristic of the Type A personality is an extreme desire for advancement and recognition. When this is lacking, hostility and anger are the usual responses. He needs to achieve because, even though on the surface he appears to be self-assured and secure, inwardly his basic feeling is one of insecurity. Another problem is that once he has achieved a goal, there is no rest; another goal must be achieved in order to prove his value and self-worth. Inner contentment or peace is an elusive dream.

5. The Type A person is unable to relax without feeling guilty. Leisure activities do not bring relaxation. Because of this, leisure activities are overplanned and overscheduled. This creates tension for himself and for family members as well.

6. Delays or interruptions produce impatience. Type A's are impatient with themselves and others. If they see you doing a task too slowly, you will hear about it. They will interrupt you, show you a faster method, and

express irritation verbally or nonverbally while you work. They are critical of you. If they play tennis, they don't wait until you are ready before they serve. If they are taking tennis lessons, they start to anticipate how they will become a pro. They finish sentences for others, rush the waiters in a restaurant, and push the elevator button ten times even though they know it doesn't have any effect. When they come to a street corner they either violate the DON'T WALK signal or else push the button on the light at each corner, then stand between the two and cross at the first one that says WALK!

7. Type A's are involved in multiple projects with many deadlines. They overextend themselves and feel frustrated and fragmented. Their energy is drawn to many projects and their work quality is limited. Even outside of work, they take on too much.

8. There is a chronic sense of time urgency among Type A's. They have a "hurry-up" sickness, and their life becomes a rat race on a treadmill.

9. Type A people have an excessive competitive drive. They are too competitive and make decisions too fast. Because aggressive behavior is needed to remain competitive,

it is easy to move from aggressiveness to hostility, and this hostility is lurking just beneath the surface, ready to erupt like a volcano. They constantly analyze their own performance and make comparisons with the accomplishments of other people.

10. Anger and cynicism are characteristic of the Type A personality. The anger is often a free-floating type of hostility and is a permanent sense of indwelling anger. It shows itself with more and more frequency, often in response to trivial situations. The Type A person is very good at creating excuses and reasons for this constant state of irritation. He appears to have logic on his side. If he becomes angry at another driver, he can point out a "good" reason for his anger. He experiences and shows anger at life situations in which other people realize that it doesn't do any good to become angry. This anger is always ready to attach itself to almost anything, from another person's opinion to someone being slow in a line at the checkstand.

11. Workaholic tendencies are common among Type A's. The word "workaholism" owes its beginnings as well as its negative connotations to the word "alcoholism." Sometimes, however, "workaholism" is considered a virtue rather than a vice. Workaholics work

hard, but not all hard workers are workaholics. Hard workers work to gain a promotion, earn more money, or to please someone. Workaholism is an approach or an attitude toward work. The workaholic thinks about work when he is not working. He loves working! Workaholics come from all classes, sexes, and occupations, and they all have the same passion—work. Many of them are very happy. The problem is that those around them are often unhappy. Workaholics are rarely at home, and when they are they do not participate much in family affairs. It is also difficult to adjust to their schedule.

Here is a simple yes/no quiz to evaluate your response to work. Write down your answers.

1. Do you get up early, no matter how late you go to bed?

2. If you are eating lunch alone, do you read or work while you eat?

3. Do you make daily lists of things to do?

4. Do you find it difficult to "do nothing?"

5. Are you energetic and competitive?

6. Do you work on weekends and holidays?

7. Can you work anytime and anywhere?

8. Do you find vacations "hard to take"?

9. Do you dread retirement?

10. Do you really enjoy your work?[9]

If you answered "yes" to eight or more questions, you may be a workaholic. There are several standard characteristics of workaholics. These traits are as follows:

They are intense, energetic, competitive, and driven. They enjoy what they do. They wake up in the morning and can't wait to get started. They drive themselves and compete with other people. Often workaholics compare among themselves the number of hours they work per week.

They have strong self-doubts. You would not suspect this to look at them, for they cover it well. They suspect that they are inadequate, so they work hard to compensate. As someone said, "He trades sweat for talent." The way they overcome their self-doubt is by doing more.[10]

Consider the following recommendations.

1. If you are a Type A or live with one, there is unhealthy anger in the environment.

2. Type A's can change *if they want to change*.

3. At the heart of the problem for a Type A is an identity self-image issue. This is where the Type A should begin with himself.

I recommend the following books.

Welcome Stress, by William D. Brown, Compcare Publications.

When I Relax I Feel Guilty, by Tim Hansel, David C. Cook Publishers.

The Sensation of Being Somebody, by Maurice Wagner, Zondervan.

Making Peace with Your Past, by H. Norman Wright, Revell.

Type A Behavior and Your Heart, by Meyer Friedman and Ray H. Rosenman.

Treating Type A Behavior And Your Heart, by Meyer Friedman and Diane Ulmer.

Much has been written about the Type A person but little attention has been given to the Type B individual. Type B's live very creative and interesting lives. They do not have an overwhelming sense of time urgency, but they do achieve results. They feel secure enough not to have to rush or live their life on a deadline basis. When working with others, they delegate authority easily and allow the individuals to do tasks in their own unique way.

One of the main characteristics of these individuals is the fact that they do not have free-floating hostility. They are not angry people. Why is this? Because they have a high degree of self-esteem. They do not have to engage in a struggle to bolster their own self-esteem by being critical of others. Type B's work just as hard as Type A's, but if they fail at their task, their self-esteem does not suffer. It is intact and is not dependent upon their performance.

It appears then that one of the answers for not just the Type A person but for anyone plagued by constant anger is building a strong sense of self-esteem upon a proper base. What can you do then at this point? Again I would refer you to the book *Treating Type A Behavior and Your Heart*, by Meyer Friedman and Diane Ulmer. In particular, see chapters 2, 3, 10-13.

9

RESULTS OF ANGER

What are the results of anger? Are they constructive or destructive? If they are destructive, do they have to be? How does anger affect one's body? How does it affect family life?

Anger motivates a person to hate, wound, damage, annihilate, despise, scorn, disdain, loathe, vilify, curse, ruin, demolish, abhor, abominate, desolate, ridicule, tease, kid, get even with, laugh at, humiliate, goad, shame, criticize, scold, bawl out, irritate, beat up, fight, compete with, crush, offend, or bully another person. All of these are definitely negative!

The first time we see the effects of anger in Scripture, they are very destructive. "But for Cain and his offering He had no regard. So Cain became very angry and his countenance fell. Then the Lord said to Cain, 'Why are you angry?' '' (Genesis 4:5,6a NASB).

Cain was angry at his brother because Abel's sacrifice was acceptable and his own was not. Inwardly Cain experienced anger, and the result was murder (Genesis 4:8). Cain was alienated from his brother, from other people, and from God. His anger led to murder and to extreme loneliness.

In another instance in Scripture we find an example of a father who, because of his displaced anger, almost killed his son. Saul was angry, envious, and jealous of David. The Scripture describes the scene: "Then Saul's anger burned against Jonathan, and he said to him, 'You son of a perverse, rebellious woman! Do I not know that you are choosing the son of Jesse to your own shame and to the shame of your mother's nakedness?' . . . Then Saul hurled his spear at him to strike him down" (1 Samuel 20:30, 33a NASB).

One of the results of anger is violence toward family members. It occurred in the Scriptures and it occurs every day in our society. Police receive more calls for family conflicts than they do for aggravated assault, murder, and all other serious crimes put together. Over 60 percent of the homicides committed in our nation are against family members. Even the police departments are concerned about responding to calls for family conflicts because 26 percent of police fatalities occur while handling family disturbance calls!

One Christian writer described the results of anger in her own life:

> I remember blaming everyone else. It was never my fault. I only started screaming after someone else had provoked me. I staunchly maintained my innocence and was very defensive about the whole matter. I lived out each day in anger. I was mad at God, mad at myself, mad at others, and fit to be tied with the angry frustrations of life in general.
>
> Anger, during those disastrous beginning years of our marriage, wrote its name across my face in hard, dark, indelible lines. . . . I was in my early 20's but my face was aging at an alarming rate!
>
> What anger did to my looks, however, was nothing compared to the atrocities it perpetrated on my emotions and my mind. Every outburst of temper took its unbelievable toll on my character and personality.
>
> As a woman, I became close-minded and opinionated about everyone from the butcher to the girls in the P.T.A. I made instant judgments and assumptions on everything from convenience foods to politics.[11]

Paul Hauck says that reacting with anger is like throwing a cactus at someone with your bare hands; he may get hurt, but so will you!

Another result of anger is that you become a carrier of a very infectious germ—anger itself! If you respond in anger, others around you can easily catch the germ. Very few people have a natural immunity to it. Anger expressed tends to multiply anger.

What kind of an example do we set for our spouse, children, employees, or friends by the kind of anger we display? Your spouse is responsible for his or her own emotional responses, but you still modeled the response. Perhaps if you respond with a kind but firm response, your spouse would follow that example instead.

10

ANGER AND YOUR BODY

Have you ever considered what happens to your body when you experience anger? Many physical changes occur. Sugar pours into the system, creating energy. Your blood pressure increases, your heart beats faster, and blood containing needed nourishment circulates more rapidly through your body. Your blood clots much more quickly than normal. Additional adrenaline is released. The pupils of your eyes dilate, mobilizing you for action. Your muscles tense up—in fact, the muscles at the outlet of the stomach can squeeze down so tightly that it is difficult for anything to leave your stomach while you are angry. The digestive tract can become so spastic that severe pains are felt during or after the time you are angry.

Your blood pressure may increase from 130 to 230. Your heart beats faster, often up to 220 or higher. People have had strokes during a fit of anger because of the increased blood pressure. During anger, the arteries of the heart can squeeze down hard enough to produce angina pectoris or even a fatal coronary attack.

Dr. Leo Madow states:

> Hemorrhage of the brain is usually caused by a combination of hypertension and cerebral arteriosclerosis. It is sometimes called apoplexy or stroke and may have a strong emotional component, as is shown by such expressions as "apoplectic with rage" and "Don't get so mad, you'll burst a blood vessel!" Anger can produce the hypertension which explodes the diseased cerebral artery, and a stroke results. Not only does repressed anger produce physical symptoms from headaches to hemorrhoids, but it can also seriously aggravate already existing physical illnesses.[12]

What happens when this anger is not released? Your body remains prepared for action. Your heart is still beating rapidly, your blood pressure is still up, and chemical changes in your blood are still taking place.

11

HANDLING ANGER

One of the best reasons for not getting angry is that anger actually prevents a person from solving problems. It simply shows that you are out of control. It is not a solution to frustration but a reaction to it. If your spouse is after you to work on your marriage relationship or spend more time with the children, the solution is to talk about it. Find out how your spouse really feels, and do as much as you can to enhance your marriage relationship.

If you don't like your working conditions, you need to either attempt to improve the working atmosphere, or else learn to live with an undesirable but not intolerable situation, or else look for another job. Getting angry in either setting will not bring about positive, lasting improvements in which all parties are satisfied.

One way of dealing with anger is to approach it from the perspective of frustration. If anger has been brought about by frustration, it will have a tendency to disappear if the frustration is removed. If a man is angry because a planned fishing trip may be suddenly canceled, he will tend to quiet down if he is able to take that trip. If you are angry because a child is not responding to your attempts at discipline, your anger will subside when he begins behaving. The point to remember is that the energy of anger does not have to be unleashed in a manner that will hurt or destroy. Instead it can be used in a constructive manner to eliminate the frustration. If the original frustration cannot be eliminated, many individuals learn to accept substitute goals and thereby find nearly as much and sometimes even greater satisfaction.

Becoming hateful and desiring revenge is only a short step beyond being angry. Anger is usually accompanied by thoughts of how to get even with the other person instead of how to love that person and help him respond in a positive and beneficial way. How can we make a friend out of someone who is angry at us? Reacting with anger is like pouring gasoline on a fire that is already blazing. A chemical retardant would be far better! Proverbs 15:1 illustrates an appropriate response:

"A gentle answer turns away wrath, but a harsh word stirs up anger" (NASB).

The other person's anger may not be turned away immediately, but in time it will happen. Remember that you will have to plan your verbal and nonverbal response to this person well in advance and even practice it if you expect it to happen. If you wait until you are in the heat of the crisis you will not (and cannot because of physical changes) be able to change your old angry way of reacting. Visualizing and practicing the Scriptural teaching in advance prepares you to make the proper response.

Why do you become angry at your family members when they don't respond to you? Why do you get angry at the kids when they don't pick up their room, mow the lawn, or dry the dishes properly?

Anger expressed by yelling at a son who does not mow the lawn carefully does not teach him how to do it correctly. Angry words directed to a sloppy daughter do not teach her how to be neat! Step-by-step instruction (even if it has been given before) can help solve the problem.

Proverbs 22:24,25 illustrates this principle:

"Make no friendships with a man given to anger, and with a wrathful man do not associate, lest you learn his ways and get yourself into a snare" (AMP). "A man of wrath stirs up strife, and a man given to anger commits and causes much transgression" (Proverbs 29:22 AMP).

12

JESUS AND ANGER

Jesus Christ experienced anger in His life, and for good reason. Norman V. Hope in *How to Be Good and Mad* gives some examples of Christ's anger.

> The Gospel records make it perfectly plain that He could, on occasion, feel blazing anger and, feeling it, could and did give emphatic expression to it. For example, in Mark chapter 3 the story is told of His healing a man with a withered hand on the Sabbath. When some protested that it was altogether improper to heal a man on the Sabbath, Jesus was indignant at their stubbornly perverted sense of values. The Scripture says that He "looked round about on them with anger, being grieved for the hardness of their hearts." In Matthew 23, the account is given of Jesus' blasting the scribes and Pharisees, whom He describes as "hypocrites" for the

revolting contrast between their high religious profession and their low, irreligious practices. And in John 2 it is recorded that Jesus cleansed the Temple of its money changers, insisting that His Father's house must not be made a house of merchandise.[13]

Jesus experienced anger and felt free to let it show. He clearly and constructively expressed His anger.

13

CONSTRUCTIVE ANGER

It should be obvious from these examples that anger is not necessarily bad. The results of anger can be either positive or negative, constructive or damaging.

Anger is like gunpowder which, depending upon how it is directed, can blast away at injustices or kill and maim the innocent.

When used constructively, anger can sometimes be an asset to a person. One who is angry enough may be able to accomplish great feats of strength which he would not otherwise be able to handle, such as raising a car off a loved one who is trapped underneath. Leo Madow in *Anger—How to Recognize and Cope With It* tells the story of a woman whose anger actually helped her function better.

She had been called as a witness in a trial and was terrified at the prospect of being interrogated. Before she was called to the witness stand, she described her brain as being a "sack of mush" and she was not sure she would be able to remember her own name. Meanwhile, the witness ahead of her in the case was saying things which were not true. As the woman listened to the testimony she became angrier and angrier. When she went on the stand, her mind was as sharp as a steel trap. She was able to testify very accurately, recalled many details that she was not aware she had known, and made a most effective witness. As she explained afterward, she became so angry at the lies of the previous witness that she forgot all her fears. . . .

Constructively used, anger can give strength both physically and mentally. Such normal outlets for anger are dependent on several factors. First, the individual must not be overwhelmed by his anger, because he is then rendered ineffective. Second, there should not be so much fear of anger that it cannot be released directly, as it will then come out in unhealthy ways. Third, opportunities for some socially acceptable outlet must exist.[14]

Ephesians 4:26 tells us to "be angry and sin not" (KJV). The word "angry" in this verse means an anger which is an abiding and settled habit of the mind, and which is aroused under certain conditions. You are aware of this kind of anger and it is under control. There is a legitimate reason for this anger.

Your reasoning powers are involved, and when reason is present, anger such as this is proper. The Scriptures not only permit it but on some occasions *demand it!* Perhaps this sounds strange to some who have thought for years that all anger is wrong. But the Word of God does state that *we are to be angry*, as explained by Spiros Zodhiates in *The Pursuit of Happiness.*

> This, then, immediately disposes of the idea that the meek are passive persons who never get angry. There is no passivity in meekness. When the Lord Jesus Christ comes into our hearts, He does not go to sleep and put us to sleep. He becomes aggressively active within us.
> . . . a Christian does and should get angry. But he must be careful to get angry at the right things and refrain from getting angry at the wrong things. Before he was saved and became blessed, his anger was sinful. Now, it must be righteous. Meekness is the sanctification of anger. It includes patience and long-suffering for personal affronts, with the willingness to speak out vigorously in defense of the Gospel. To get angry at what we should and when we should is a definitely Christian characteristic.[15]

As Dr. J. H. Jowett says:

> A life incapable of anger is destitute of the needful energy for all reform. There is no

blaze in it, there is no ministry of purification. If a city is to be purged from its filth it will have to be by souls that are burning with moral resentment. It is the man who is "fervent in spirit" who will most assuredly "serve the Lord." "The grass withereth... because the Spirit of the Lord breatheth upon it." The Church needs more of this withering breath and consuming energy that is born of holy wrath against all established wrong. We are taught in the New Testament that this power of indignation is begotten by the Holy Spirit. The Holy Spirit makes us capable of healthy heat, and it inspires the fire within us. The Holy Spirit never creates a character that is lukewarm, neutral, or indifferent.[16]

Paul actually commended the Corinthians in one place for their aroused indignation against the believer who had married his own mother (1 Corinthians 5:1,2; 2 Corinthians 7:11).

This is righteous anger. It is not sinful when it is properly directed. Such anger must be an abiding, settled attitude of righteous indignation against sin, coupled with appropriate action.

There are three main characteristics of righteous anger. First of all, it must be controlled. It is not a heated, unrestrained passion. Even if the cause is legitimate and is directed at an injustice, uncontrolled anger can cause an error in judgment and increase the difficulty. The mind must be in control of the emotions so that the ability to reason is not lost. "Be angry and sin not." Perhaps the way this is accomplished is related to the Scriptural teaching in Proverbs: "Be slow to anger." This kind of anger is not a direct result of immediate frustration.

Second, there must be no hatred, malice, or resentment. Anger that harbors a counterattack only complicates the situation. Perhaps our best example of how to respond is Jesus' reaction to the injustices delivered against Him.

"When He was reviled and insulted, He did not revile or offer insult in return; [when] He was abused and suffered, He made no threats [of vengeance]; but He trusted [Himself and everything] to Him Who judges fairly" (1 Peter 2:23 AMP).

"Beloved, never avenge yourselves, but leave the way open for [God's] wrath; for it is written, Vengeance is Mine, I will repay (requite), says the Lord" (Romans 12:19, AMP).

The final characteristic of righteous anger is that its motivation is unselfish. When the motivation is selfish, usually pride and resentment are involved. Anger should be directed not at the wrong done to oneself but at the injustice done to others.

It is possible to confront another person without being excessively angry. We need not confuse anger with confrontation and firmness. Anger usually springs from a desire to defend ourselves or to get someone to do what we want. You can share your feelings of frustration over the very same things, but in a nonviolent, nonattacking manner. When we are angry, we can simply state the fact calmly that we are angry.

14

YOUR CHOICES

Once a person discovers he is angry, how can he deal with that anger? What choices are available to him? There are four basic ways to deal with anger.

Repression

One way is to *repress* it: Don't even admit that you are angry; ignore its presence.

This repression is often unconscious, but is *not healthy!* Repressing anger is like placing a wastebasket full of paper in a closet and setting fire to it. The fire will either burn itself out *or* it could set the entire house on fire and burn it down. The energy produced by anger cannot be destroyed. It must be converted or directed into another channel.

One outlet for repressed anger is accidents. Perhaps you have met people who are *accident-prone.* Unfortunately, their accidents may involve other people as well as themselves. A man who is angry may slam a door on his own hand or someone else's. He may wash windows for his wife when he would rather be watching a game on TV, and put his hand through the window. Perhaps his driving manifests his anger when he "accidentally" runs over the rose bushes.

Repressed anger can easily take its toll on your body by giving you a vicious headache. Your gastrointestinal system—that thirty-two foot tube extending from the mouth to the rectum—reacts beautifully to repressed anger. You may experience difficulty in swallowing, nausea and vomiting, gastric ulcer, constipation, or diarrhea. The most common cause of ulcerative colitis is repressed anger. Repressed anger can affect the skin through pruritus, itching, and neurodermatitis. Respiratory disorders such as asthma are common effects, and the role of anger in coronary thrombosis is fairly well accepted.[17]

Dr. Wallace C. Ellerbroek, a program director at Metropolitan State Hospital at Norwalk, California, says, "Learned control of such thoughts is much more important in prevention of heart disease than is strict adherence to a low-cholesterol diet."

In an exclusive interview he also stated that

"miserable people have high cholesterol but happy people do not."

> If you check coronary victims, he contends, you'll find they were either depressed or angry before their coronary. Cholesterol does play a role in heart disease, he explains, but it is bad emotions, not diet, that send cholesterol levels soaring.
>
> For example, he likes to cite a study of Navy flight cadets. On the mornings the cadets were scheduled to fly, their cholesterol ranged from 400 to 650—extremely high. But on the mornings they didn't have to fly, their cholesterols were 140 to 165—in other words, entirely normal.
>
> Any negative emotion—anger, depression, frustration, irritation, unhappiness, the blues—is going to affect the entire body and brain adversely to some degree.[18]

Anger and hatred can lead to further complications. But so does repression. Repressed anger, or anger held in or turned inward, often turns into depression. In our unconscious attempt to handle the emotion, we bring harm to our own body.

Jonah is a classic example of a man whose anger turned inward. He was sent by God to warn the people of Nineveh about their sinfulness. He completed this task successfully to the point where the King of Nineveh turned from his sin and commanded his people to do likewise. In turn God "abandoned his plan to destroy them and didn't carry it through" (Jonah 3:10 TLB).

The Biblical record goes on to say: "This change of plans made Jonah very angry. He complained to the Lord about it: 'This is exactly what I thought you'd do, Lord, when I was there in my own country and you first told me to come here.... For I knew you were a gracious God, merciful, slow to get angry, and full of kindness; I knew how easily you could cancel your plans for destroying these people. Please kill me, Lord; I'd rather be dead than alive....' Then the Lord said, 'Is it right to be *angry* about *this?*' So Jonah went out and sat sulking on the east side of the city" (Jonah 4:1-5 TLB).

However, all does not go well with Jonah; depressed, he sits under a vine. The vine dries up, and the heat from the sun becomes intense. Then in a last recorded dialogue with God, Jonah states, "It is right for me to be angry enough to die!" (Jonah 4:9 TLB). *Anger turned outward made Jonah desire Nineveh's destruction.* Then he sought the cooling comfort of the vine, and *his anger turned inward and became depression.* At one point Jonah was content just to sit and "hole up," and at another point he wished for, and asked for, death.

As David Augsburger writes in *Seventy Times Seven*:

> Repressed anger hurts and keeps on hurting. If you always deal with it simply by holding it firmly in check or sweeping it under the rug, without any form of release or healing, it can produce rigidity and coldness in personality.
>
> Even worse, hostilities pushed down into the depths of consciousness have a way of fermenting into other problems: depression, anxiety, and eventually mental breakdown.
>
> Or repressed anger may come out indirectly in critical attitudes, scapegoating or irritableness. Often those we call "good people" who harbor hostility will do indirectly and unconsciously what "bad people" do directly and deliberately, because unreleased, buried anger colors their motive.[19]

Many large manufacturing companies dispose of their industrial waste material by pumping it into underground mines or abandoned wells. This works for a while, but eventually it can pollute water systems or even burst out into the open through another channel. Our repressed anger is our own unrefined waste material.

Dr. William Menninger said:

> Do not talk when angry but after you have calmed down. Sometimes we push each other

away and the problem between us festers and festers. Just as in surgery, free and adequate drainage is essential if healing is to take place.[20]

Joseph Cooke describes what happened to him when he internalized his anger.

Squelching our feelings never pays. In fact, it's rather like plugging up a steam vent in a boiler. When the steam is stopped in one place, it will come out somewhere else. Either that or the whole business will blow up in your face. And bottled-up feelings are just the same. If you bite down on your anger, for example, it often comes out in another form that is much more difficult to deal with. . . .

For years and years of my. . .life, I worked to bring my emotions under control. Over and over again, as they cropped up, I would master them in my attempt to achieve what looked like a gracious, unperturbable Christian spirit. Eventually, I had nearly everybody fooled, even a measure of my own wife. But it was all a fake. I had a nice-looking outward appearance; but inside, there was almost nothing there. . . .

The time came when the whole works blew up in my face, in an emotional breakdown.

All the things that had been buried so long came out in the open. Frankly, there was no healing, no recovery, no building a new life

for me until all those feelings were sorted out,
until I learned to know them for what they
were, accept them, and find some way of
expressing them honestly and nondestruc-
tively.[21]

Anger is an emotion that must be recognized
and accepted. "When you repress or suppress
those things which you don't want to live
with," suggests John Powell in *Why Am I
Afraid to Love?* "you don't really solve the
problem because you don't bury the problem
dead—you bury it alive." God created us with
the capacity for emotional reactions. We need
to recognize and accept our anger for what it
is. Only then can we learn to use it wisely and
properly.

Suppression

A similar way to handle anger is to *suppress*
it. A person choosing this means is aware of
his anger but chooses to hold it in and not let
people know he is angry. In some situations
this may be healthy and wise, but eventually
the anger needs to be recognized and drained
away in a healthy manner. Otherwise the
storage apparatus will begin to overflow at the
wrong time and place. The person who *always*
stuffs anger away is a sad case. The constant
effort of holding it back results in an incred-
ible waste of energy.

Though their cheerful, smiling exteriors make it seem otherwise, "stuffers" are usually very unhappy people. Some stuffers literally stuff themselves by eating enormous amounts of food, partly as a way of punishing themselves for the sin of anger.

Often a person chooses to suppress his anger when the person with whom he is angry could react with more force or authority than he can. For example, an employer calls in one of his employees and angrily confronts him about some alleged problem. The employee feels his own anger rising but realizes that if he expresses his anger to his boss he could lose his job. So he suppresses his anger—until he arrives home. His wife greets him when he walks in the door and he replies with an angry snarl. This surprises her, and she will either react by snapping back at him or by suppressing her own anger. But then her teenage son walks in and she vents her pent-up anger upon the unsuspecting boy. He takes out his anger on the younger brother, who in turn kicks the dog, who bites the cat, who scratches the three-year-old, who takes out her frustration by pulling off the head of her Barbie doll! This simple process of directing your anger on a less threatening person is called *displacement*. It may help you for the moment, but it can set up a long-lasting chain of events that infects the lives of other people like an epidemic.

Guilt is another reason for displacing anger. If you are furious with your mother but believe that it is wrong to get angry with one's mother, you may find yourself exploding at other older women. Or you may use displacement to avoid humiliating yourself. You are traveling with your husband and trying to make mileage on a particular day. You take a wrong turn and go 50 miles in the wrong direction. You then project the blame onto your husband and accuse him of misguiding you.

Is the cause for your anger realistic? Is it reasonable? Is it born out of frustration? Does it come from unexpressed desires? Deal with the problem directly. If you have a disagreement with your employer over office procedures, the solution is not to go home and complain to your wife or to another employee. Talk with him directly and attempt to resolve the problem. If this is not practical, then you must put up with the situation and find other constructive outlets for your anger when it arises. The ideal solution is to practice various responses to your frustration.

If the cause for your anger is not legitimate, the problem is within you. If you get angry with your wife because she does not cook meals the way your mother did, then you had better recognize first of all that your wife is not your mother! Allow her to develop her own cooking skills and to try some new recipes. Then learn to compromise on some of your expectations.

Dr. James Dobson was once asked the question, "Many psychologists seem to feel that anger should be ventilated or verbalized. They say it is emotionally and physically harmful to repress or withhold any intense feeling. Can you harmonize this scientific understanding with the Scriptural commandment that 'every man [should] be swift to hear, slow to speak, slow to wrath' (James 1:19 KJV)?" His response was very helpful:

> I do not find these objectives to be in contradiction. God does not want us to repress our anger—sending it unresolved into the memory bank. Why else did the apostle Paul tell us to settle our irritations before the sundown each day, effectively preventing an accumulation of seething hostility with the passage of time?
>
> But how can intense negative feelings be resolved or ventilated without blasting away at the offender—an act which is specifically prohibited by the Scripture? Are there other ways of releasing pent-up emotions? Yes, including those that follow:
>
> By making the irritation a matter of prayer.
> By explaining our negative feelings to a

mature and understanding "third party" who can advise and lead.

By going to an offender and showing a spirit of love and forgiveness.

By understanding that God often permits the most frustrating and agitating events to occur, so as to teach us patience and help us grow.

By realizing that no offense by another person could possibly equal our guilt before God, yet He has forgiven us; are we not obligated to show the same mercy to others?[22]

It is interesting that some psychologists today advocate cutting loose with all your anger regardless of the way you do it or the results. But other psychological research in the past few years indicates negative results of ventilating all of one's anger. The findings show that as the level of verbal aggression increases (anger poured out), the level of physical aggression increases dramatically. Discussing things calmly, getting information bearing on the issue, and calling for help from outsiders helps to settle the problems and keep the possibility for physical violence lower.[23]

Suppressing anger does have some merit, however, especially if it helps you relax, cool down, and begin to act in a rational manner. The Word of God has something to say about this type of suppression.

"He who is slow to anger has great understanding, but he who is hasty of spirit exposes and exalts his folly" (Proverbs 14:29 AMP).

"A hot-tempered man stirs up strife, but he who is slow to anger appeases contention" (Proverbs 15:18 AMP).

"He who is slow to anger is better than the mighty, and he who rules his own spirit than he who takes a city" (Proverbs 16:32 AMP).

"Good sense makes a man restrain his anger, and it is his glory to overlook a transgression or an offense" (Proverbs 19:11 AMP).

"Make no friendships with a man given to anger, and with a wrathful man do not associate" (Proverbs 22:24 AMP).

"A (self-confident) fool utters all his anger, but a wise man keeps it back and stills it" (Proverbs 29:11 AMP).

"Let every man be quick to hear . . . slow to speak, slow to take offense and to get angry" (James 1:19 AMP).

The individual who practices and exerts self-control will find that his anger level actually decreases. He will not become as angry as if he were to simply cut loose with his first reaction. A calm consideration of the cause for the anger and the results will help you handle the situation properly.

Elizabeth Skoglund says:

> Christ himself was slow to anger with the woman caught in adultery because he knew her heart, and he reacted quickly against her accusers because he also knew their inner thoughts. He showed anger at the disciples when they tried to keep the children from him, and yet he was tender when the multitudes pressed against him. In violent anger he chased the money changers out of the temple, but he showed only a weary disappointment when the disciples slept while he prayed in the Garden of Gethsemane.[24]

Jesus experienced anger and felt free to let it show. He clearly and constructively expressed His anger.

Expression

Expressing your anger is a third way to handle it. Some people think you should express exactly how you feel no matter what or who is involved. They feel this is psychologically healthy and necessary in order to live a balanced life.

There are many different ways to express anger. One is to react with violent passion, yelling harsh words and swearing with tremendous emotion. This can bring results, but you may not care for them. If you are allowed the freedom to react this way, shouldn't the other person have the same freedom to react to you in the same way?

But you can also express your anger by riding your bike around the block, digging in the garden for an hour, or beating on a stuffed pillow. These people are called "doers." You can write down exactly how you feel when you get angry, especially if it is difficult to verbalize your feelings. These methods may sound strange, but they should not be discounted. They have been used to help many people overcome their difficulties with anger.

If both you and your spouse are angry, it is better, if you are working it off physically, to do it separately. For some reason the anger disappears faster.

What habitual doers need to keep in mind, however, is that while hitting a tennis ball or polishing a floor may make them feel better, these activities are seldom directly related to the source of anger.

Everyone can and probably should be a doer some of the time, but if your only way of handling anger is to escape into physical activity, ask yourself the following questions from time to time: At whom am I angry, and why? How can I change things and feel better?

Confession

"The final method of dealing with anger is to *confess it*. This is...the best method, especially if it is coupled with an intelligent and healthy use of suppression or self-control. Confess the fact that you are angry—to yourself, to God, and to the person involved. Don't say, 'You're making me angry.' The individual is not making you angry; you are responsible for your own emotional reaction toward him. You could say, 'The way our discussion is going, I'm getting angry. I'm not sure that's the best reaction, so perhaps we could start over in our discussion.' Or, 'I'm sorry, but I'm angry. What can I do now so we can resolve our differences?' Try admitting and confessing your anger."[25]

Confession used in this sense does not mean that the anger is sinful. It means admitting and facing your anger. Another way of saying this is to possess and process your anger. Accept its presence and your responsibility for being angry, and do something about it in a constructive way.

Elizabeth Skoglund says:

Remember, Christ does not condemn anger. For the Christian problem of feeling anger should never be spiritualized. The mother who feels anger at her son's low grades at school is not sinful nor does that anger have to be confessed as sin. The young man unjustly or even justly released from his job does not sin when he feels anger. Anger is a natural reaction to pain. What we do with that anger, however, may have profound spiritual implications.[26]

What about talking things over while you are still angry? Doesn't this help? Actually it is very difficult to talk rationally about problems when you are angry. Exercise or relaxation is important before people attempt to resolve their differences. When people are calm, results are more evident. Confession and time may be the proper steps in the right direction. Just the admission of being angry can help you release the feeling and get the message across in an acceptable manner to the person involved.

David Augsburger writes about the problem in *Caring Enough to Confront*:

Explosive anger is "the curse of interpersonal relations." Vented anger may ventilate feelings and provide instant, though temporary, release for tortured emotions, but it does little for relationships.

Clearly expressed anger is something different. Clear statements of anger feelings and angry demands can slice through emotional barriers or communications tangles and establish contact.[27]

15

OTHER PEOPLE'S ANGER

"My biggest problem," John said as he sat quietly near me, "is that I don't know what to do or how to act when others get angry with me. I either withdraw and crawl into a cocoon or I explode viciously. Neither response solves the problem!"

You and I will always live around people who become angry with us. Here are some suggestions for handling their anger and our own.

1. Give the other person permission in your own mind to be angry with you. It is all right. It isn't the end of the world, and you can handle it. Say to yourself, "It's all right for them to be angry. I can handle it."

2. Do not change your behavior just to keep the other person from being angry with you. If you do, you are allowing yourself to be

controlled. If someone else becomes angry it is his or her responsibility to deal with it.

3. Do not reward the other person for becoming angry with you. If the person yells, rants, and raves, and you respond by becoming upset or complying with what he or she wants you to do, you are reinforcing his or her behavior. If the person is angry but reasonable, respond by continuing to state your point in a caring, logical manner.

4. Ask the person to respond to you in a reasonable manner. Suggest that he or she restate the original concern, lower his or her voice, and speak to you as though you had just been introduced for the first time.

5. If another person is angry, you do not have to become angry also. Read back over the Scriptures listed earlier, and apply them to your life.

If anger interferes with communication between you and your spouse, there are ways you can change the pattern.

Identify the cues that contribute to the anger. It is important to determine *how* and *when* you express anger. What is it that arouses anger? What keeps the anger going? What is it that you do in creating the anger and keeping it going? Focus only on your part; don't lay any blame on your partner.

One way to accomplish this is by the use of a behavioral diary. Whenever anger occurs, each spouse needs to record the following:

1. The circumstances surrounding the anger, such as who was there, where it occurred, what triggered it, etc.
2. The specific ways you acted and the statements you made.
3. The other person's reactions to your behaviors and statements.
4. The manner in which the conflict was eventually resolved (if at all).

Develop a plan of action for interrupting the conflict pattern. This plan should involve immediate action to disengage from the conflict. It should also be a way to face and handle the problem at a later time. Interrupting the conflict is an application of Nehemiah 5:6,7: "I [Nehemiah] was very angry when I heard their outcry and these words. And I consulted with myself, and contended with the nobles and the rulers" (NASB).

Even the neutral expression of the phrases "I'm getting angry," "I'm losing control," "We're starting to fight," or "I'm going to write out my feelings" is a positive step. Upon hearing one of these statements, the other person could say, "Thank you for telling me. What can I do right now that would help?"

A commitment from both of you not to yell

or raise your voices and not to act out your anger is essential. We call this "suspending" the anger. Agree to return to the issue at a time of less conflict. Most couples are not used to taking the time to admit, scrutinize, and then handle their anger.

The interruption period could be an opportune time for you to focus upon the cause of your anger.

David Mace suggests two additional positive ways to control your anger.

> This does not mean you do not have a right to be angry. In an appropriate situation, your anger could be a lifesaver. Anger enables us to assert ourselves in situations where we should. Anger exposes antisocial behavior in others. Anger gets wrongs righted. In a loving marriage, however, these measures are not necessary. My wife is not my enemy. She is my best friend; and it does not help either of us if I treat her as an enemy. So I say, "I'm angry with you. But I don't like myself in this condition. I don't want to want to strike you. I'd rather want to stroke you." This renouncing of anger on one side prevents the uprush of retaliatory anger on the other side, and the resulting tendency to drift into what I call the "artillery duel." If I present my state of anger against my wife as a problem I have, she is not motivated to respond angrily. Instead of a challenge to fight, it is an invitation to negotiate.

Ask the other person for help. This step is the clincher. Without it, not much progress can be made. The anger may die down, but that is not enough. Both individuals need to find out just why one got mad at the other. If they do not, it could happen again, and again, and again. Your request for help is not likely to be turned down. It is in the other person's best interest to find out what is going on, and correct it if a loving relationship is going to be maintained.[28]

If you have certain behaviors that tend to provoke anger in other people, you should eliminate the behaviors so they have no reason to retaliate. Even defensive behaviors can be a trigger.

Change the faulty thinking pattern that affects the relationship. Here again the problem of expectations and assumptions arises. The faulty beliefs will need to be exposed and challenged. Some common themes are:

"You won't love me if I tell you how I really feel."

"You won't love me if I disagree with you."

"It's better just to hide how I feel."

"It's better just to fake it and go along with what he wants."

"Even if I do speak up, you'll win anyway."

"He should know what I need."

"All anger is wrong, so I'm not going to express any."

Analyze and challenge the assumptions and eliminate any mind-reading.

Redirect your focus from "Who is right or wrong?" to "What are the behaviors involved, and how do they affect our relationship?"[29]

16

AGGRESSIVE VERSUS ASSERTIVE ANGER

Anger can be either aggressive or assertive. One style of aggressive anger is being loud and boisterous. The feelings are expressed at a high decibel level. When frustration is so high, some people feel that shouting is the only way to make their point. Still others get their body into action by flapping their arms, gesturing with their fist, kicking, or stomping their feet. It is very easy for this anger to cross the line into violence. Hitting the wall, the door, or the other person is the final result of this emotional outburst.

Recently a client and his wife came into my office for their weekly visit. Something was new—a cast on his right hand. I thought of joking with him and saying, "How did you break your hand? Hitting the wall?" But fortunately I didn't ask the question. We proceeded through the session, and just before we closed I asked, "What happened?"

"Well," he said, "with all the upset and financial frustrations and the hassle around the home the other night, I was so angry and frustrated that I slugged the wall. Unfortunately, the wall didn't give, and I knew right away by the pain that I broke a bone. I guess I learned that hitting something is not the best way to deal with my anger."

When people go on and on with their anger in this way, unless they hit a wall and break a bone, there is a tendency to keep the anger going. Self-control has flown away like a bird in flight, and reasoning with this person at this time is futile.

Another demonstration of aggressive anger is caustic, critical comments. These people express themselves in ways that put others down. Blame is often used, as is sarcasm. They really do not have a desire to resolve the issues. The anger has a bite and a sting to it, and it is meant to be felt by the receiver.

Such anger leaves the other person feeling totally frustrated, irritated, and disarmed. This approach does not resolve the problem, but is an invitation for continued warfare. This choice of avoiding open conflict causes bad feelings to fester and grow.

Les Carter makes an interesting distinction between aggressive and assertive anger. Aggressive anger he defines as the emotion exhibited by persons who make a firm stand for their own convictions without demonstrating a concern for the needs of others. Assertive anger, on the other hand, is the emotion exhibited by persons who take a firm stand for their own convictions while at the same time being considerate of the needs of all involved.[30]

Types of Anger

Aggressive	*Assertive*
Seeks to punish a person who does wrong.	Seeks to help a person who does wrong.
Does not care about the other person's point of view.	Tries to be discreet and understanding.
Is hard-nosed, immovable, and demanding.	Is firm, yet willing to seek alternatives.
Is condemning and judgmental.	Recognizes that all people have faults.
Has high expectations of everyone.	Knows that even the finest people are fallible.
Cares more about what happens to self.	Is concerned about self and others.
Holds grudges.	Knows the value of forgiving.
Hates to admit one's own areas of weakness.	Recognizes that everyone can be in a state of self-improvement.[31]

One of the most basic principles to follow in dealing with your anger is this: Try to cut off your anger at the earliest possible moment. The trigger point is the best place. But there are actually four different stages at which you can deal with your anger:

1. You can deal with your anger when you are calm. This is the best possible time to prepare yourself so you don't experience anger unnecessarily. Ask yourself—

    • Do I make unnecessary demands upon myself? On others?
    • Do I set up unrealistic demands for myself? For others?

The realities of life are that people do make mistakes, children do misbehave, and spouses do sometimes forget and are inconsiderate. If you can begin to accept as a fact of life that you and others are imperfect, your anger will lessen.

Write out how you would like to respond when irritations and annoyances occur. Then take the time to practice this new approach in your mind. Here is an example of such an exercise.

If there is a situation or person who is constantly proving to be a source of irritation, picture yourself taking the action necessary to deal with the problem. Talk to the person involved and see if the two of you can remove the source of irritation. You may find it helpful to plot on the following chart the anger you usually feel.

Date	Time	Intensity of Anger	What I Become Angry At
		Light High 1 2 3 4 5	
How I Respond			How I Want to Respond

If you can see a pattern to your anger, could you do something to break that pattern?

2. The second possibility is to cut off the anger before it begins. No one is 100 percent consistent, and there will be times when your anger breaks through. But planning for a new response when you are not angry can help. It is possible to cut off your anger by becoming aware of the possible onset of anger. Two ways of doing this are identifying what other people do or say that makes you angry and identifying the self-talk you use to create anger. Then write out substitute statements

which will stop your self-talk from producing anger.

_____

_____

_____

_____

_____

_____

_____

_____

_____

_____

_____

Ask yourself again and again, "Do I need to get angry?" Pretend that you are in a court of law and are the jury. Could you really convince a jury that you need to get angry? Remember, you have a choice whether to become angry or not. Just knowing that you are responsible for this decision may have some effect upon your response.

3. A third stage at which you can deal with anger is when you are actually angry. First, recognize and accept your anger. To resolve

it, you need to admit and recognize it. Often we hear angry people shout, "I am *not* angry!" It may help to accept another person's evaluation of what is taking place. Assume that you are angry.

The next step is give up your desire to strike back. If you are angered because you have been hurt, you will usually want to hurt back. In fact, not only do we want to hurt back, but we want to punish and make the person pay for what we think he has done. Romans 12:17-19 states, "Never pay back evil for evil. Let your aims be such as all men count honourable. If possible, so far as it lies with you, live at peace with all men. My dear friends, do not seek revenge, but leave a place for divine retribution" (NEB). If we carry our anger it becomes resentment.

One of my clients had a tendency to erupt over even the smallest irritation and disruption by his employees. Since he owned the business, there was little the workers could do. He was aware of his explosive nature and wanted to learn to respond differently. He was also a man who liked to be in control of his life and everything around him. He was a bit taken back when I said, "How does it feel to allow other people and situations to control you?" He replied, "What do you mean, control me! I'm in control of my life."

"Well," I said, "on the one hand, you've

said these other people and situations and interruptions make you angry. If they do, don't they control you? If, on the other hand, you are in control of your life, you could choose not to respond in this angry manner.''

He was stunned and silent. Eventually he admitted that he was in charge of his emotional responses. We then proceeded to work out a system of both delaying and short-circuiting his anger response and also a system for warning others that he might be in a bad mood. He went out and purchased small flags and placed them on his desk. Whenever he was in a good mood or handling responses fairly well, the green flag would be flying. If he started to become upset or at the first anger response, the green flag would be lowered and replaced by the yellow caution flag. Then when he was really angry and upset, the red flag would be raised. I was amazed at the effect of this visual reminder.

After one month the green flag had not been lowered once. My client said, ''It's amazing how much the flag reminds me that I don't have to become upset and angry. This is something that can be controlled. And my staff appreciates both the warning system and the effect it's had on me already.''

4. ''Conscious delay'' is a procedure which can be used to hold back angry or negative

responses which have been generated in the mind. It is possible to edit negative thoughts (which is not the same as denying or repressing them) so that you will express yourself or behave in a positive manner. It is not hypocritical or dishonest to edit your thoughts. Ephesians 4:15 states that we are to speak the truth in love. A literal translation of this verse means that we are to speak the truth in such a way that our relationship is cemented together better than before. Totally blunt, let-it-all-hang-out honesty does not build relationships. By editing, you are aware of your thoughts and feelings and you are also controlling them. You are actually taking the energy produced by the anger and converting it into something useful which will build the relationship.

How is it possible to edit your thoughts when you begin to become angry? First of all, make a list of some of the behaviors of your spouse (or another person) which you respond to with anger. Here are some examples:

• My spouse is usually late, as much as 15 or 20 minutes. Whenever this happens I become angry.

• My spouse frequently overspends the monthly household allotment and doesn't tell me about it.

• My spouse leaves clothes and dishes

around the house consistently and expects others to pick them up.

• Often when I set up an outing or a date for us (even well in advance) my spouse has already planned something for that time and doesn't tell me in advance.

Now list the statements you make to yourself about each statement. What are some of the possible explanations for the way the other person is behaving? What are three alternate statements you could make to your spouse to replace your usual response?

All of us, at one time or another, use a variety of self-talk statements which tend to generate anger. David Burns describes some of these in his book *Feeling Good: The New Mood Therapy.*

There are numerous occasions when anger is caused by distorted thinking. As a person learns to replace distorted thoughts with realistic thoughts, irritability lessens and self-control increases.

What are the kinds of distortions which occur most frequently when anger exists? One main offender is *labeling*. When you describe a person you are mad at as "a klutz" or "stupid" you see that person in a negative way. When you label a person, you also give the impression that he or she is a bad individual. You direct your anger toward what you think that person "is."

If you write off a person in this way, you catalog in your mind everything you don't like about him or her (which is a mental filter) and discount or ignore his or her good points (disqualifying the positive). In doing this we create a false target for our anger.

Labeling is a distorted thinking process. It causes a person to feel morally superior or inappropriately indignant, or both. It is a way of building one's own self-image at the expense of someone else. Labeling makes it easy for us to blame another person toward whom we feel a need to retaliate. Labeling can also become a self-fulfilling prophecy.

Mind-reading is another type of thinking which generates anger. It's very simple: We invent motives which explain to our own satisfaction why another person did what he or she did. But we are dealing with a false premise, since our hypotheses do not describe the actual thoughts that motivated the other individual. And we probably do not take the time to check out what we are saying to ourselves about the other person.

Another form of anger creating distortion is magnification. Whenever a negative event is exaggerated, your emotional reaction may be blown out of proportion. You're driving on the freeway and the traffic comes to a halt. Five minutes later it is still at a standstill. You begin saying to yourself (or out loud!) "I can't take this! I can't stand this!" But isn't that an exaggeration? Aren't you taking it? Aren't you sitting there stuck in traffic experiencing what everyone else is experiencing? Since you are taking it, why tell yourself you aren't? You can take the delay. Why not give yourself credit for sitting there? Your only other alternative is to get out of your car and start walking. But not too many people leave their cars sitting on the freeway while they walk away.

One of the most important elements involved in reducing anger is to develop the *desire* to stop your anger. Once you are angry, it is difficult to stop the process of taking a verbal bite out of the other person. The desire for revenge which frequently accompanies anger can be consuming. But there is a way to short-circuit this anger: Make a list of the advantages and disadvantages of being angry and acting out of revenge. It is important to consider both the short-term and long-term consequences of anger. After the list is compiled, review it and ask, "Which are greater, the costs or the benefits of anger?" This usually helps a person realize that there is a better way to respond than with anger and revenge. In addition to listing the advantages and disadvantages, go one step further and list the positive consequences that might result from not becoming angry.

David Burns tells how this process helped one of his clients named Sue. Sue had two daughters from a previous marriage, and her husband, a hardworking lawyer, had a teenage daughter from his previous marriage. Since John's time was limited, Sue tended to feel deprived, angry, and resentful. She was bitter because John was not being fair to her in giving her enough time and attention. She then proceeded to list the advantages and disadvantages of her anger and concluded with a list of the possible positive consequences of not becoming angry. Here is the way her list looked.

Advantages of My Anger	Disadvantages of My Anger
1. It feels good.	1. I will be souring my relationship with John even more.
2. John will understand that I strongly disapprove of him.	2. He will want to reject me.
3. I have the *right* to to blow my stack if I want to.	3. I will often feel guilty and down on myself after I blow my stack.
4. He'll know I'm not a doormat.	4. He will probably retaliate against me, since he doesn't like being taken advantage of either.

5. I'll show him I won't tolerate being taken advantage of.

5. My anger inhibits both of us from correcting the problem that caused the anger in the first place. It prevents resolution and sidetracks us from dealing with the issues.

6. Even though I don't get what I want, I can at least have the satisfaction of getting revenge. I can make him squirm and feel hurt like I do.
Then he'll have to shape up.

6. One minute I'm up, one minute I'm down. My irritability makes John and the people around me never know what to expect. I get labeled as moody and cranky and spoiled and immature. They see me as a childish brat.

7. I might make neurotics out of my kids. As they grow up, they may resent my explosions and see me as someone to stay away from rather than to go to for help.

8. John may leave me if he gets enough of my nagging and complaining.

9. The unpleasant feelings I create make me feel miserable. Life becomes a sour and bitter experience, and I miss out on the joy and creativity I used to prize so highly.[32]

The possible consequences of not becoming angry were:

1. People will like me better. They will want to be near me.

2. I will be more predictable.

3. I will be in better control of my emotions.

4. I will be more relaxed.

5. I will be more comfortable with myself.

6. I will be viewed as a positive, nonjudgmental, practical person.

7. I will behave more often as an adult than as a selfish child.

8. I will influence people more effectively.

9. My kids, husband, and parents will respect me more.[33]

If you really would like to control your anger, keep a journal and list those irritating situations which seem to plague you. Take the time each day to evaluate those situations, and then reread what you have written. You may be surprised at the controlling effect of this procedure. But be sure you continue to do this day after day. Even when we would like to make a small positive behavioral change in our lives, it will take a minimum of 18 repetitions over a period of 18 days before it becomes a habit.

Our thought life is critically important to the way we live. In some way our thoughts are translated into bodily changes that can cause such reactions as anger, anxiety, fear, irritability, etc. Paul said, " . . . bringing into captivity every thought to the obedience of Christ" (2 Corinthians 10:5 KJV). If some thoughts are not controlled, they create other thoughts. They are like rivers which in turn create tributaries; one thought leads to another.

One way to improve the content of your self-talk is to monitor it. Here is one suggestion to help you become aware of your internal conversations.

1. Each hour check your thoughts. Set an alarm or use some device to alert you every hour.

2. When you signal yourself, stop whatever you are doing and review the thoughts you have been experiencing. What was the conversation you were having with yourself? Write down your thoughts in a sentence. What statements were you making which contributed to your anger or to being upset? What were the sentences?

3. Review each sentence by asking yourself these questions:

- Is it true?
- How do I know it is true?
- Where is the evidence?
- Am I overreacting?

- Will this be true 12 hours from now?
- What is another possible response?
- What are the consequences of this path of thinking?
- Now counter any negative self-talk with positive, realistic statements.

You can also use the emotion of anger to monitor and capture your thoughts. This is a bit more difficult because you will have to interrupt the emotional response of anger as soon as you feel it beginning to arise.

When you first begin to experience an emotional reaction, stop and label it. This helps you admit to yourself what you are feeling. Write it down. It could be "I am irritated," "I'm angry," "I'm angry and I wish something would happen to that person," or "I'm upset."

The second step is to ask yourself, "Why am I feeling this way?" Remember that your emotional responses are messages. They are trying to signal you about the cause. At this point be sure to give as many reasons as possible.

The third step is to identify the thoughts which led to your present feeling. Was there a chain of ideas that led to the emotion? What were the statements?

The last step is to take all your thoughts which you wrote down during the day and review them. Compare them with your thoughts on other days. Is there a trend in your thinking? What changes would you like to make in your thought patterns at this time?

17

MENTAL REHEARSAL AND IMAGERY

Anger is swift and eruptive and occurs in episodes. Because of its eruptive nature, anticipatory preparation or mental rehearsal is a key factor in changing anger responses.

In the space provided below, indicate in order of importance the five most anger-creating situations you currently experience.

1. _____

_____

_____

_____

2. _____

_____

_____

_____

3. _____

_____

_____

_____

4. _____

_____

_____

_____

5. _____

_____

_____

_____

Now use the process of imagery. Close your eyes and imagine yourself becoming angry as you are accustomed to doing. Hear the statements you usually say to yourself. See yourself responding in anger in your usual way. Feel the emotion of anger in your body.

Now take a minute to relax and imagine yourself in the same situation, but this time make rational, calm statements to yourself. See yourself responding in the way you would like to respond. See yourself putting into practice the Scriptural guidelines of "being slow to anger." Feel yourself responding in a relaxed and calm manner. Hear yourself making calm, balanced statements. Did you experience the difference? You will be able to change your angry reactions if you spend time in advance visualizing yourself responding in the desired fashion.

Practice your new version of the experience in your mind again and again until you feel comfortable and competent. When the real situation confronts you, a new response is possible. Now take each of the angry situations you have identified and go through the same process you have just completed. The way other people respond is not that important. If they respond in a positive manner, that's fine. If they respond in a negative manner, that's fine also. Your anger or lack of anger is not dependent upon the other person's responses. Consistent practice will help you become more proficient and relaxed about responding in this new and more positive manner.

Don't you have to be angry in order to get your point across? Some people don't seem to respond unless anger is a part of the message! Believe it or not, it is possible to share a complaint or a criticism with another person in a calm, well-thought-out manner that will bring about *more* change than if you responded to him in anger. Many couples find the lack of healthy problem-solving to be a major area of dissatisfaction in their marriages. Here are a few techniques which have worked for some people. Perhaps these will help you avoid an angry explosion.

1. State the problem or complaint as soon as you can verbalize it. The longer you let the problem fester, the greater the possibility of resentment building and bitterness eroding the relationship.

2. Share your problem or concern in private so you don't embarrass the other person or cause him to feel that he must save face.

3. Let the person know that you are pleased with several aspects of the relationship before sharing what it is that bothers you.

4. Be sure to speak in the first person. Use "I statements" such as "I feel" and "I don't like to be" rather than "you are" and "you did this." "You statements" sound like accusations and quickly lead to self-defense and nonlistening, and perhaps even counter-complaining.

5. Pinpoint the actions that concern you; don't become a mind-reader focusing upon what you *think* the other person's motives are. Perhaps he was rude or didn't listen, but do you really *know* that he had definitely planned to do that?

6. Comparing this person's actions and behavior with those of other people does little to help solve the problems you are concerned about.

7. Forget the past. Talk about the present issue and make no reference to past difficulties.

8. Share only one complaint. It is too easy for the other person to feel dumped upon if he or she receives a barrage of problems all at the same time.

9. Be sure to suggest in a nonangry, nondemanding, nonjudgmental way some of the possible and realistic solutions that could be implemented.

10. Be sure you let the other person share his feelings and ideas about the problem that you are bringing to his attention. Even if he responds in anger to what you have said, his response is no reason for you to become angry. [34]

You can approach the other person by saying something like, "John, I have a problem. I'd like to talk with you about it because our relationship is important to me, and this may help me. I feel. . . ." After you share in this nonjudgmental manner be sure to ask, "What do you think?"

The Scripture says that a "soft answer turns

away wrath." It also says that I am to be "slow to anger." Perhaps you're responding, "I know it *says* that, but how can I *do* it? I have these people at work who every now and then get angry with me and start chewing me out with some complaint. I do get angry. How can I respond to them in a healthy way that would also be consistent with the teaching in the Bible?"

Remember that just because someone is upset with you, you don't have to become upset yourself, no matter what he says or how he says it. Here are some suggestions for responding to angry statements.

1. If someone has a criticism to make of you, stop what you are doing and look directly at him. By giving your attention directly to him, the irritation may be lessened.

2. Listen to the person; let him talk. Proverbs 18:13 says, "He who answers a matter before he hears the facts, it is folly and shame to him" (AMP). Try to hear what the person is really saying. Try to hear what is behind his remarks. You may just be the object of all of his pent-up frustration, with nothing personal intended.

3. Accept the criticism as the other person's way of seeing things. From his perspective, his interpretation is correct. And he could be right, so don't write off the complaint. If he

exaggerates, don't get hung up attempting to correct him at that time.

4. Don't accuse the person of being over-sensitive or easily irritated. That won't help solve the problem that has been presented.

5. Don't bring up another subject or attempt to evade the present issue. Don't joke about the complaint either, because it could be very important to the other person.

6. Be open to the criticism and consider its validity before you respond. It could be right, and this could be an opportunity for you to grow. You could even thank the person for bringing it to your attention. Consider the following passages in Proverbs from The Living Bible before you make your response.

"If you refuse criticism you will end in poverty and disgrace; if you accept criticism you are on the road to fame" (13:18).

"Don't refuse to accept criticism; get all the help you can" (23:12).

"It is a badge of honor to accept valid criticism" (25:12).

"A man who refuses to admit his mistakes can never be successful. But if he confesses and forsakes them, he gets another chance" (28:13).

7. After the person has finished sharing his

complaint with you, ask for an opportunity to respond to what he has said. First, restate what you heard the other person saying to show that you were listening and to make sure you understood everything. Then share what you feel and believe, and if the other person is correct, be sure to admit it. If you feel he is mistaken, you could defend yourself. How you share your feelings is very important.[35]

18

WHAT IS YOUR ANGER SAYING?

What is the answer to controlling and channeling your anger? What is your anger saying to you? What is its message? Could it be expressing a deeper hurt or desire? Behind angry looks could be fear and rejection. Underneath feelings of anger could be concealed expectations and subsequent frustrations. Inside angry statements could be hidden demands. David Augsburger suggests both a cause and a solution.

> You see, hostility has its root in reaction to love that is withheld or denied.
> The only cure, then, is in filling that void with love. God offers love. Unconditional love that will fill an open heart and heal the hurts.
> When you open your life to the love of God, you are unreservedly accepting God's love and God's loving way of living for yourself.

Then the love of God goes to work penetrating the depths of your spirit with healing.

A second step in opening your life to God is to absorb not only the assurance of His love and His loving spirit within you, but His Word. Read the Bible. Mull it over. Let it soak down deep into your mind. Memorize it. There is power in stocking your memory and your heart with what is lovely, good, wholesome, true.[36]

19

STEPS FOR HANDLING FRUSTRATION AND ANGER

Here is a summary of the techniques we have discussed which you can use to handle your anger and frustration.

1. Describe the behavior or attitude that you want to change (anger, quarreling, yelling, etc.).

_____

_____

_____

2. List several personal reasons for giving up this behavior or attitude.

_____

_____

_____

_____

3. Your own motivation to change is very important. From your reasons for giving up the behavior or attitude, select the most important reason. Write it down.

_____

_____

4. Begin to think about how you should change your behavior if you wish to succeed. Write down these ideas.

_____

_____

_____

_____

5. Adopt a positive attitude. What has been your attitude toward anger in the past? Describe it. Indicate what attitude you are going to have now. How will you maintain this new attitude? Write down your answers to these questions.

_____

_____

_____

_____

_____

_____

6. When you eliminate a behavior or attitude that you dislike, a vacuum or void will often remain. Frequently a person prefers the old behavior to this emptiness, so he reverts back to the previous pattern. In order for this not to happen, substitute a positive behavior in place of the negative one. Describe what you can substitute for the behavior or attitude that you are giving up.

_____

_____

_____

_____

_____

_____

7. Read the Scriptures again that are listed for this problem area (see below). List the positive behavior or attitude that these Scriptures suggest in place of the negative ones. Write out the way you see yourself putting each particular Scripture into action in your life. Describe how you picture yourself actually doing what the Scriptures suggest. Describe the consequences of thinking or behaving in this new way.

Here is a passage of Scripture to use for

practice. (Many have found this passage very applicable to their lives and circumstances.)

Example
Ephesians 4:31-32

Behavior or attitude to **STOP**	List the results of this behavior. Give several results for each one.
Bitterness (resentfulness, harshness)	
Anger (fury, antagonism, outburst)	
Wrath (indignation, violent anger, boiling up)	
Clamor (brawling)	
Slander (abusive speech)	

Positive Behavior or Attitude to **BEGIN**	*What do you think would be the results of obeying these three commands? List several results for each.*
Kindness (goodness of heart)	
Tenderheartedness (compassion)	
Forgiveness (an action)	

Now write out the practical ways in which you see yourself doing the things suggested in the verse. Write down when and how you will begin and the consequences that you expect. Be very specific.

_____

_____

_____

_____

_____

_____

_____

_____

_____

_____

_____

Now consider the following Scriptures that pertain to your area of concern and write down your response to each verse.

Ephesians 4:26

Proverbs 15:1

Proverbs 15:18

Proverbs 16:32

Proverbs 19:11

Proverbs 29:11

DISCUSSION SUGGESTIONS

1. What do you feel most frustrated about?

_____

_____

_____

_____

2. What does God want you to do with your emotions?

_____

_____

_____

_____

_____

127

3. Show others how you look when you're angry.

4. Describe how you feel when you're angry.

_____

_____

_____

_____

_____

_____

5. How do you handle guilt in your life?

_____

_____

_____

_____

_____

_____

6. What makes you feel really good about yourself?

_____

_____

_____

_____

_____

_____

7. What do you think God feels about you?

_____

_____

_____

_____

_____

8. What are some things that we as Christians should be angry about?

_____

_____

_____

_____

_____

_____

9. What do you think is the best way to handle your anger?

_____

_____

_____

_____

_____

10. Read Proverbs 15:1. Give examples of this verse in action. How can a person be consistent in following this passage?

_____

_____

_____

_____

_____

11. Read Proverbs 22:24, 25. What do you think this means for a family?

_____

_____

_____

_____

_____

12. Describe how you can be "angry and sin not" (Ephesians 4:26 KJV).

_____
_____
_____
_____
_____

13. If you were honest and expressed your anger, how would the other members of your family react?

_____
_____
_____
_____
_____

14. List as many causes for anger as you can.

_____
_____
_____
_____
_____
_____

15. Scripture says, "Be slow to anger." Describe how this can be done.

_____

_____

_____

_____

_____

GROUP QUESTIONS AND ACTIVITIES

(Use some or all of these ideas, depending on the time available.)

1. Begin by asking everyone to write his or her own definition of anger. (Provide paper and pencils.) Ask for several persons to give their definitions. Share your definition last. (3-5 minutes.)

2. Provide every person with a blank piece of paper and with several crayons of various colors. Ask them to draw a symbolic picture of how they feel when they become angry. When everyone has completed this, ask for some volunteers to show their drawings to the class, but do not have them explain the drawings. Ask for some opinions and observations from others as to the meaning of the drawings. Then have those who drew the pictures explain what they represent. (15 minutes.)

3. Break into smaller groups of four or five to discuss these two statements. Ask each group to find Scriptural teachings that answer each of these statements: 1) It is a sign of spiritual and emotional immaturity for a Christian to be angry with another person; 2) Scripture teaches that we should avoid people given to anger. (7 minutes.)

4. Describe the effect of anger upon the body. Use material presented earlier in this book. Read the story of Nabal in 1 Samuel 25 and expand upon that event. (5-10 minutes.)

5. Ask the group to discuss Ephesians 4:26: "Be angry and sin not" (KJV). Form small groups of three to discuss how a Christian can be angry and not sin. Ask each group to come up with specific examples. (10 minutes.)

6. Provide paper and pencil for everyone. Ask each person to write down the answers to these questions:

a. Describe the kind of anger that you usually experience, using the Biblical descriptions of anger.

b. How do you express this anger?

c. What can a person do to make himself "slow to anger?"

After they have had time to write their answers, ask for volunteers to share their answers with the entire group. Start with Question c, then ask for answers to Questions a and b. (20 minutes.)

7. Share various methods of dealing with anger. (5-10 minutes.)

8. Discuss the principles for dealing with anger as expressed in this book. (5-10 minutes.)

9. Provide paper and pencils. Ask members to read Proverbs 15:1 and 29:11 and write out how they visualize themselves putting this passage into practice in their everyday lives. After everyone has done this, break into small groups of three or four and ask everyone to share his or her answers. Then ask for some to share their responses with the entire group. Some may want to role-play what they have determined to do. (30 minutes.)

10. Close the session by reading Philippians 4:9, which emphasizes the concept of practice. Encourage the class to take the

time this week to find other Scriptures that deal with anger, and to follow the same procedure of writing out and then visualizing the Scriptures as a vital part of their lives.

NOTES

1. Paul A. Hauck, *Overcoming Frustration and Anger* (Philadelphia: Westminster Press, 1974), p. 65.

2. Harold Blake Walker, *Power to Manage Yourself* (New York: Harper & Brothers).

3. Gary R. Collins, *You Can Profit from Stress* (Santa Ana: Vision House Publishers, 1977), p. 39.

4. Charles R. Swindoll, *Growing Strong in the Seasons of Life* (Portland: Multnomah Press, 1983), pp. 163-64.

5. Richard P. Walters, *Anger, Yours and Mine and What to Do About It* (Grand Rapids: Zondervan Publishing House, 1981), p. 17.

6. Ibid., p. 139.

7. Neil Clark Warren, *Make Anger Your Ally* (New York: Doubleday, 1983), p. 22.

8. Paul A. Hauck, *Frustration*, p. 86.

9. Marilyn Machlowitz, *Workaholics* (Menlo Park, CA: Addison Wesley Publishers, 1980), pp. 17-20.

10. H. Norman Wright, *A Marriage for All Seasons* (Santa Ana: Christian Marriage Enrichment, 1982), pp. 26-27.

11. Joyce Landorf, *The Fragrance of Beauty* (Wheaton: Victor Books, 1973), pp. 108-9.

12. Leo Madow, *Anger—How to Recognize and Cope With It* (Totowa, NJ: Charles Scribner's Sons, 1972), p. 85.

13. Norman V. Hope, "How to Be Good and Mad," in *Christianity Today*, July 19, 1968.

14. As quoted in H. Norman Wright, *The Christian Use of Emotional Power* (Old Tappan, NJ: Fleming H. Revell, 1974), pp. 111-12.

15. Spiros Zodhiates, *The Pursuit of Happiness* (Grand Rapids: Wm. B. Eerdmans Publishing Co., 1966), pp. 263-64.

16. As quoted in Zodhiates, *Pursuit*, pp. 270-71.

17. Wright, *Marriage*, pp. 121-22.

18. Wallace C. Ellerbroek, "Anger-Sorrow Can Cost Your Life," in the *Long Beach Independent Press-Telegram*, Jan. 24, 1973, p. 60.

19. David Augsburger, *Seventy Times Seven* (Chicago: Moody Press, 1970), p. 60.

20. William Menninger, "Behind Many Flaws of Society," in *National Observer*, Aug. 31, 1964, p. 18.

21. Joseph R. Cooke, *Free for the Taking* (Old Tappan, NJ: Fleming H. Revell Company, 1975), pp. 109-10.

22. James Dobson, *Dr. James Dobson Talks About Anger* (Glendale: G/L Publications, Regal Books Division, 1975), pp. 16-17.

23. Murray Straus, "Leveling, Civility and Violence in the Family," in *Journal of Marriage and Family*, Feb. 1974, pp. 13,21.

24. Elizabeth Skoglund, *To Anger with Love* (New York: Harper & Row, 1977), p. 89.

25. Wright, *Marriage*, p. 127.

26. Skoglund, p. 89.

27. David Augsburger, *Caring Enough to Confront* (Glendale: G/L Publications, Regal Books Division, 1973), p. 49.

28. David R. Mace, "Marital Intimacy and the Deadly Love-Anger Cycle," in *Journal of Marriage and Family Counseling*, Apr. 1976, p. 136.

29. H. Norman Wright, adapted from *More Communication Keys for Your Marriage* (Ventura, CA: Regal Books, 1983).

30. Les Carter, *The Push-Pull Marriage* (Grand Rapids: Baker Book House, 1983), p. 62.

31. Ibid., p. 63.

32. David Burns, *Feeling Good* (New York: Signet, 1981), pp. 141-44, 149-50.

33. Ibid., pp. 149-51.

34. Adapted from John Lembo, *Help Yourself* (Niles, IL: Argus Communications, 1974), pp. 40-41.

35. Adapted from Lembo, *Help Yourself*, pp. 42-43.

36. Augsburger, *Seventy Times Seven*, p. 62.